Gianni, Jan & Marcello Liscia

WORKBOOK
RESPONSIBILITY

Showing responsibility for decisions made, for employees and for oneself

Illustrations:
Herman Reichold

Responsibility is the second of five books in the D.R.E.A.M. of LEADERS® publication series.

Bibliographic information of the The German National Library: The German National Library lists this publication in the German National Bibliography; detailed bibliographic data can be found on the website at http://dnb.dnb.de.

1ˢᵗ edition 2018

Imprint
© 2018 Gianni, Jan & Marcello Liscia

Layout, cover + worksheets: Franziska Eikel, Liscia Consulting
English translation by Ramey Rieger: doitwritetranslations@gmx.de

Text + Layout:
Biographiewerkstatt Böddeker
Ellerstraße 26 – 33100 Paderborn
Telephone: 05293 - 9327816

Print and publishers: : Books on Demand, Norderstedt
ISBN: 978-3-7528-5825-9

Table of Contents

Preface   7

Employees' quality of life   **11**
Worksheet: Your company's needs   21

Perpetual motion – story changing®   **23**
Worksheet: Which transitional changes are you going through now?   33

Cultivating physical and mental resources   **35**
Worksheet – Test: Am I a burn-out candidate?   45

Making decisions   **48**
Worksheet: Tetralemma – A decision-making method   56

Sustainability   **58**
Worksheet: Your principles   61

The Authors   65
Keynote presentations for your event   66
One 'n' Herman, the artist   67

> *"You are not only responsible for what you do,*
> *but for what you don't do as well."* [1]
>
> Lao Tzu (Chinese philosopher)

Dear Reader,

Thank you for choosing our second workbook addressing the topic of Responsibility. Perhaps you have already read our book *D.R.E.A.M. of LEADERS® Leadership is not an Illusion* as well as our other four workbooks.

Should that not be the case, and you're now wondering what this *D.R.E.A.M. of LEADERS®* actually is, then let us fill you in. For more than 15 years, Liscia Consulting promotes people, guiding them in their professional development. For us, there is no greater honor. Thus, we have made cultivating leaders our primary responsibility, most specifically, by developing the D.R.E.A.M. Formula[2]:

D Dedication: Wholehearted commitment to mission, 24 hours a day
R Responsibility: Assuming full responsibility for your decisions, for your staff and for yourself
E Education: Ensuring you and your staff evolve
A Attitude: Living and communicating your personal mindset (philosophy) and values
M Motivation: Commitment as the foundation of all deeds

The D.R.E.A.M. Formula acronym can also be understood as a checklist, illustrating the self-concept of a leader. It is how leadership can be understood and lived. This is a highly complex and many-layered topic. Thus, our book, *D.R.E.A.M. of LEADERS® Leadership is not an Illusion* could render but a

---

[1] Unspecified quotes are taken from *Book of Quotations* (Bassermann-Verlag, 2013) or from digital quote collections.

[2] D.R.E.A.M.-Formel® is a protected trademark owned by Liscia Consulting and registered with the German Patent and Trademark Office.

first impression of our understanding of leadership. In the meantime, we have published a separate workbook to each of the letters in the D.R.E.A.M. Formula, going further into certain aspects, providing more examples and worksheets at the end of each chapter for practical application of knowledge gained. The workbooks are intentionally structured to be used independently of the first book. The chapters' basic structure has been maintained, expanded with additional examples. So, reading the other books is not a prerequisite to working with this one.

This workbook goes into a leader's responsibility for his employees' quality of life and how he can fulfill this responsibility during transitional processes, with the aid of *story changing*®. A leader is also responsible for his own mental and physical resources, as well as those of his workers. The final chapter addresses sustainability.[1]

We wish you enlightening enjoyment reading and learning!

Ciscia.Jie: _Jau lime_ _Marcelle fixig_

---

[1] To enhance readability, we have alternated masculine and feminine non-specific personal pronouns per chapter. Hence, in this context, we consider both genders gender-neutral and hope they are understood as such.

Responsibility

R ⌐

LISCIA:	Do your employees look forward to the end of the workday?
CEO:	Of course! It'd be weird otherwise, wouldn't it?
LISCIA:	Do you look forward to to the end of your workday?
CEO:	Heavens, yes! I can't wait to get out of here!
LISCIA:	Too bad.
CEO:	Huh?

Employees' quality of life

Our concept of a leader is someone who makes a decisive contribution to his employees' well-being in a variety of day to day professional areas. Let us look at this more closely.

An important aspect of this responsibility is the employees' quality of life. This is a broad topic, so we would like to focus on one example often cited on our sector, as it aptly and concisely describes problems surrounding the work-life balance. A leader should design a work environment in which co-workers look forward to going home each evening – as opposed to looking forward to finally getting off work. What may look like a case of semantic dogmatism at first glance, makes all the difference when viewed up close.

Certainly, it is completely normal and understandable to look forward to quitting time. It is also important to be able to truly relax and enjoy leisure time. An employee perceiving her work as nothing but a permanent strain because, for example, she is caught in a dysfunctional trust relationship with her boss who leaves her no leeway for self-expression, will get up in the morning loathing her job and bring that aversion to work with her. There, she concentrates on getting through the day instead of focusing on the work at hand, wishing the hours would go by faster so she can finally go home.

This situation quickly becomes a vicious circle. The employee leaves her work-place frustrated. She cannot recollect having achieved anything satisfying or successful over the past hours. Quite the opposite. She goes home feeling thwarted and disgruntled, making it hard to enjoy the leisure time she so longed for at work. Her energy is devoured by thoughts revolving around her vexing work situation and eventually she will be too exhausted to make appropriate use of her free time. Just as a negative work environment can make a co-worker's private life miserable, a satisfying workday can enrich employees' leisure time. We all know times of stress and strain, but the satisfaction of masterfully overcoming obstacles, and having this feeling mirrored by superiors and colleagues, is not only an excellent motivator the following work day, it also charges us with energy for our private lives.

The endocrinologist Hans Selye coined the terms *eustress* and *distress* to describe these two conditions. He defined eustress as a physical-emotional state arising from positive challenges. Eustress is beneficial to body and soul. i.e. positive stress. It is diametrically opposed to distress, which debilitates the organism, with long-term exposure leading to complete exhaustion (burnout syndrome).[1]

Thus, it is more than gratifying when, at the end of a stressful but basically satisfying day at work, your employees look forward to going home. They leave with a feeling of achievement, bringing positive energy to their free time. These co-workers don't try to shut out the workday, that would be a waste of energy. They shift into their other roles in life. They are no longer managers, engineers or production directors, they are husbands, wives, fathers, mothers and/or club members.

Here, we are often asked if it is not important for a person to be able to shut down. And, certainly, it is important to be able to shut down your organism, but first when you are finished with your day – not your workday. It's a case of linguistic precision. At the end of the working day, a person should be able to shift their energies toward family and leisure activities. Only when the day is done, and they go to bed, then a person should shut down completely. If they were to shut down directly after work, why bother to go home at all?

The provocation in the last question is intentional. It illustrates the profundity of a leader's responsibility to his employees. She must ensure their well-being; see to it that their work is fun and interesting and that they come to work gladly. Employees who feel unwelcome at work or feel their jobs are just a necessary evil, will not feel well at home, either. And this, in the long run, will have a very negative impact on their work performance.

---

[1]   Cf. zeit.de, *Wir! Sind! Super!* / *We! Are! Super!*, 13.10.2016

In his book, career consultant Martin Wehrle expresses this as follows, "We love to spit out the words work-life balance, even though it's nonsense. If work and life are two separate entities, then that would mean when we are at work, we are dead! [...] Anyone laying in a work coffin for eight hours a day, will hardly be able to wash off the smell of decay at the end of the day. An unhappy professional life quickly becomes an unhappy private life."[1]

Assuming responsibility for employees is not always an easy issue to communicate. Every now and then, it takes stronger language to get the point across. Thus, a few years ago, while coaching a leader in the engineering field, we said to him, "You know what? Your best bet would be to give each of your employees a punching bag for Christmas." "Why on Earth would I do that?" the man asked in amazement. "To spare their kids a beating. Because that's what is going to happen if you don't change your attitude. Your workers are going to go home and beat up their children."

Our words were visibly a shock to the man. And of course, they weren't the opening words we spoke upon initiating his coaching. We had already approached him with several similar messages, couched in much milder terms. But there are moments when it takes someone fearless enough to deliver a verbal slap in the face. And fearlessness is one of our major assets.

And that wasn't the end of it. We made it perfectly clear, "When one of your employees comes home from work, charged with anger and looking for a scapegoat, you are responsible. When he beats his children, it's actually you he's lighting into."

For this reason, in our leadership training we like to draw from the US American psychologist Abraham Maslow's *Hierarchy of Needs Pyramid*. "Oh no, not him again!" Some of you may be thinking, rolling your eyes, having had a bellyful of Maslow in business school or college. It's the same reaction we also meet in our training sessions. So, you think Maslow's theory is ancient history? Yes, he developed it in the mid-fifties (and expanded on it in the seventies). In our eyes, though, Maslow's theory is as topical as it gets, and we'll give you a solid example to back it up.

---

[1]   Wehrle, Martin, *Sei einzig, nicht artig / Be original, say no*, mosaik 2015, pg.292 ff.

But if you're unfamiliar with the Hierarchy of Needs Pyramid, here's its structure of five levels:

1. Basic, existential needs (physiological needs): That without which we cannot survive - air, food, drink, sleep, warmth, shelter, sexuality.
2. Security: Material and financial security, health and well-being, personal security
3. Social needs: Also known as deficiency needs, as the absence of love, family, friendship and belonging can have a debilitating impact.
4. Esteem: This need encompasses both the desire for strength, achievement and competence as well as the need for prestige, status, celebrity and power.
5. Self-actualization: The need to fulfill your potential, to develop and grow.

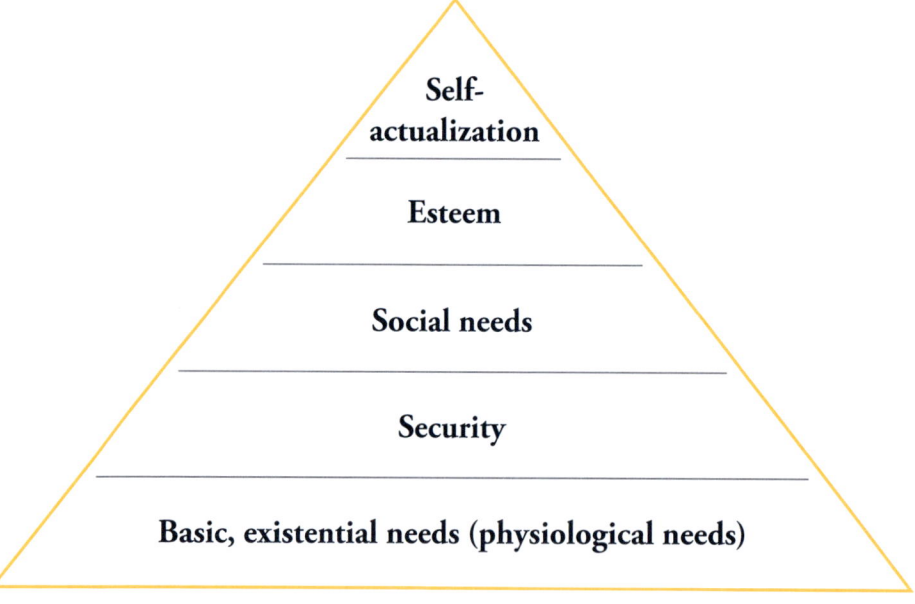

Maslow assumed that some needs take priority over others. To put it simply, we really do need air and water more than we need a new smartphone. The bottom of the pyramid shows the existential needs that must be met. The higher you travel up the pyramid, the less relevant these needs are to survival.

When viewing the pyramid as a leader, I am obligated to ensure my workers can satisfy their needs on all levels. It is a total waste of time to fiddle around on the upper levels, lecturing my staff on self-fulfillment when the existential needs such as enough sleep or time out are lacking. Especially the things we take for granted are often ignored, although precisely the so-called trivial things build the foundation for a successful, satisfied workforce. Do my employees have access to healthy foods and drinks? Is the office or production hall temperature conducive to working comfortably? How about the ergonomic design of workplaces? Only when these basic needs are sufficiently satisfied can you begin your approach to the higher pyramid levels.

Some time ago, we guided the management team of a Southern European company through the D.R.E.A.M. of LEADERS® training. A central theme was the lack of employee engagement. The managers complained that despite their efforts, their employee engagement was far from uplifting. They had installed several perks such as a talent program and a leadership academy, without noticeable results. Did we have any idea why?

Our answer, "Yes, we do. This may come as a surprise to you, but crux lies in the blatantly evident. When you step into one of your plants, no matter where it is in Europe, you're greeted with the same sad environment. It's dark, it's grey, it's depressing and it's filthy. The reek of oil follows you wherever you go. And the same is true for your offices. When was the last time you had the walls painted? Thirty years ago? The furniture is equally dilapidated. Shall we go on?"

We invited the managers to close their eyes. "Imagine this: all around you, you see nothing but grey, depressing neglect." Once they had this image, we modified it, "Now imagine these very same conditions. Not at one of your plants, but at your own home!" Their eyes opened wide in horror. "We are constantly talking about a professional homeland," we explained, "but you create a hovel. It's no wonder your employees are demotivated. They spend at least eight hours a day here. How would you feel?"

Now the decision-makers knew where to start, and before long appropriate measures were taken. Offices and production halls were renovated, including fresh paint, modern lighting and plants. Not only the workforce profited, customers and suppliers praised the new look and refreshing atmosphere.

Satisfying the Maslow pyramid basic needs had an enormous positive impact on employee engagement.

Still, we hadn't reached our destination yet. There was another step to take as we learned that several managers turned down promotions despite the development opportunities and pay raise that accompanied them. Why? We discovered that those managers working on the plant level were not obligated to travel often, meaning they could go home in the evenings. A promotion, however, would entail assuming regional responsibilities, ergo, much more travel time.

In talks with us, at least five leaders left no doubt that they would gladly move up the ladder, fulfilling their need for self-actualization (step 5 on the pyramid). But their social relationships - contact with family, friends and neighbors - would suffer from so much time away from home. Their social needs (step 3) were clearly more important than their need for self-actualization and also took priority over prestige, status and power (step 4), the other promotion perks. The company therefore needed to find another way to promote their high potential staff members without them sacrificing their social life. Isn't it possible, in our digitalized days of virtual leadership, to shape or structure a manager's future regional activities so she can uphold her social relationships without suffering a major loss of contact? Only then would the managers willingly take the next step in their careers. The lower steps on the pyramid must be acknowledged first, before the upper ones can be approached. Abraham Maslow was and is right on the money.

The consequences of consistently neglecting human needs can be truly dangerous. Imagine a pressure-cooker left on the stove. At some point it has to explode. This is why we urged the engineering manager to buy his workers a punching bag for Christmas. If they had no alternative for relieving the pressure of neglect, the punching bag could well be their children.

Speaking of Christmas, it's an excellent example of steadily mounting tension, as any parent would know. Days, or even weeks before the Big Day, children begin to grow excited and can hardly contain their suspense. The tension grows to a breaking point, finally discharging on Christmas morning when gifts are opened. An everyday example is our dog Phillip, who knows he will be fed at 7pm each evening. As early as 5pm, you can see the tension begin to rise since he knows he won't have to wait much longer.

Frustration is a result of unmet needs coupled with no options for releasing the tension. Imagine your children's faces when there are no gifts beneath the tree! Phillip would be more than frustrated if his food bowl failed to be filled at seven on the dot. But frustration is only the beginning of the spiraling plunge into disaster. A frustrated person can still be an excellent co-worker, as long as she still perceives her frustration and can still recall the satisfaction of having her needs met. Much worse is when frustration evolves into resignation; when a staff member has given up on having her needs met at all. This worker has completely forgotten what it feels like to have her needs fulfilled, all options for releasing tension have been shut down. She feels nothing. And resignation becomes apathy and/or lethargy. Trying to coach a person beaten into resignation is an enormous challenge because it is very difficult to reach her.

This issue plays a significant role in stress management and burnout prophylaxis as it has a pervasive negative influence on employees' quality of life. Not too long ago, we were training a nursing manager who had been planning her vacation for ages. Although her vacation had long been applied for and approved, the workload at the hospital left her no or very limited time to actually take it. This went on for years. "I can't even remember how it feels," she complained to us. "Recently, I had a few days and could have taken a short vacation, but somehow it felt wrong. I couldn't even relax on my couch and read a book. I just couldn't let go. Apparently, I have completely forgotten how it feels to have free time, I wouldn't know what to do with it even if I had it. So, I went to work, for lack of an alternative." Shortly thereafter she indeed went to the hospital, but this time as a heart attack patient…

This is a well-known quantity on the management level. Companies take for granted that their leaders will work 12, 14 or 16 hours a day, including weekends. Many find themselves at the airport Sunday evenings, so they can meet their customer promptly Monday morning. Most managers feel obligated to answer incoming mails over the weekend or keep their business cellphone on hand during vacation time. Altogether, this ever-ready accessibility is a huge issue when it comes to an employee's quality of life.

The mere *thought* that your cellphone *could* ring any minute, that an email *could* reach your mailbox, is enough to keep you from relaxing on the weekend or after working hours. For this reason, staffers often maintain tension levels over extensive periods of time, even during their leisure time, which inevitably leads to burnout or other afflictions. Subtly and stealthily stress increases, usually without the afflicted person even being aware of it. We will go into this further in the chapter after the next in *Cultivating physical and mental resources.*

Fortunately, albeit slowly, companies are catching on and changing their ways. Carmakers Volkswagen, Daimler and BMW as well as corporations such as Bayer, E-on and Telekom have successfully introduced varying measures that protect their employees from the perpetual digital deluge and from ceaseless accessibility.

"The good news is that more and more bosses grasp the problem. Before that, many would ask themselves, 'How could it possibly be stressful for her employees when she writes an email Sunday morning? They can respond whenever they want to!' That's pure poppycock. Your cellphone buzzes and you see on the display that it's your boss. Most staffers will want to know what she wants. They excuse themselves from the dinner table, write a short answer [...]. Thomas Sattelberger got the message, 'I used to be one of those who would send emails at all hours of the day or night.' As former CHRO of Deutsche Telekom, he installed the regulation dictating that no one was obligated to read their emails after working hours, on the weekends or on vacation."[1]

In the meantime, many companies shut down the email server connected to all employees' smartphones after working hours, booting it up again only a half-hour before work begins. Daimler went so far as to develop their own *Mail on Holiday program.*

"After the initial pilot phase, this summer all Daimler employees could have their emails automatically deleted while they were on vacation. The carmaker's workforce should return to work 'with a cleared desk,' says CHRO Wilfried Porth. 'There's no mailbox back-log, and that's an emotional relief.' The program is now available to the 100,000 Dax workers with their own mailboxes. An

---

[1] spiegelonline.de, *Deutsche Konzerne kämpfen gegen den Handy-Wahn / German corporations fight cellphone madness,* 17.02.2014

out-of-office message refers incoming posts to the current representative."[1] As early as 2010, Telekom executives had officially established the practice of not sending emails to their workers after hours, on the weekends or during vacation.

"The board of directors was shocked into awareness by reports from their competitor France Télécom, many of whose employees took their own lives, leaving suicide notes denouncing the stress and terror at work."[2]

[1] welt.de, *Daimler löscht alle Mails, die im Urlaub kommen / Daimler deletes all mails during vacation time*, 13.08.2014

[2] spiegelonline.de, *Deutsche Konzerne kämpfen gegen den Handy-Wahn / German corporations fight cellphone madness*, 17.02.2014

Key Lisciaman message
A leader is responsible for his employees'
quality of life. The alleged small needs
such as enough sleep and leisure time
must first be met before venturing
into the need for self-actualization.

Your notes

Worksheet: Your company's needs

How well do you meet your employees' needs according to the five steps of Maslow's Pyramid? Also give thought to how well your own needs are met.

1. Basic, existential needs (physiological needs): The things we need to survive – air, food, drink, sleep, warmth, etc.

_____

_____

_____

_____

_____

_____

2. Security: Material and financial security, health and well-being, personal safety

_____

_____

_____

_____

_____

_____

3. Social needs: Family, friends and a sense of belonging

_____

_____

_____

_____

_____

_____

4. Esteem: The desire for strength, achievement and competence as well as prestige, status and power

---

---

5. Self-actualization: The desire to fulfill your potential, to develop and grow

---

Which needs fall short of fulfillment?

What can you do to improve this?

LISCIA:	How have you dealt with changes in your department thus far?
CEO:	It's particularly important to us to to inform our employees as early as possible and get them on board. We are fully aware that each person reacts differently to change and that change often triggers anxiety. Of course, there are others who welcome change, but that's usually the exception.
LISCIA:	My compliments, that sounds truly commendable!
CEO:	You think so?
LISCIA:	Yes. Many leaders are not nearly so attentive. What do you think about a model depicting each employee's position in a transitional process, taking into account how he or she feels about it?
CEO:	I've never heard of such a model, but the idea is outstanding!

Perpetual motion – story changing®

As early as two thousand years ago, the Greek philosopher Heraclitus propounded that *the only constant in life is change.* Most leaders are also aware of this phenomenon, as they must fluently react to continuously fluctuating parameters on rapidly evolving markets.

Despite the omnipresence of change, most employees resist it, are often literally paralyzed by it. As Jack Welch, U.S. American manager-legend so aptly put it, "Change has no advocates – and a perceived revolution has even fewer. People cling to the status quo and you must be prepared for massive resistance." A company must be prepared for massive resistance engendered by the human factor, which can have a fast and fatal impact on transitional processes. Transitional processes also call for leaders, not managers, as experience shows that managers rarely embody the necessary empathy to guide changes – and humans respond best to empathy.

Employees want nothing more than for things to move steadily along their accustomed path, business as usual, please. It is up to leaders to be the first to adapt to changes and guide their people through them. This is an enormous responsibility. It encompasses instilling trust, providing orientation and security. It means alleviating your people's fear of the new, so they can accept the necessity of change. And there's more. Your team must assume their role in shaping the change, because only when everyone pulls together can change successfully come about – and become the next business as usual.

Be very wary, however, of making false promises. Telling employees that everyone will come out a winner when the dust has settled is a bald-faced lie. You cannot know whether someone feels like a winner or a loser. This wholly depends on the person's subjective perception. A sense of losing is not only triggered by being fired. For some, losing can just as easily mean a transferal to another department or to a different team.

Take the story a leader at an IT service provider told during a coaching session. It had taken him about a year and a half to bring a seriously ailing company department back to productive health. Just as he began to sit back and relax, pleased with his success, he was transferred to a different department in even worse condition than the one he had just saved. It took him six months to realize he was not being demoted but could actually be proud of the transferal. He eventually grasped that the change was an honor, singling him out as the best man for the job.

So, you see, only subjective perception determines whether a person is a winner or is a loser, and individual awareness is extremely difficult to measure or chart. Therefore, we developed *story changing*®, a model for visualizing the personal emotions a co-worker traverses during a transitional process. This is not about administrative guidance during change, we will go into that at the end of this chapter when we describe our *T.O.M.A.S. Principle*.[1] The *story changing*® model deals first and foremost with people and how changes impact their personal story.

A few years ago, a friend of ours from the film industry pointed out that our approach, focusing on the emotional aspects of a transition, has many parallels with the *hero's journey* stylistic device. Everyone aspires to make something of their life, yet the attachment to the familiar, to the tried and true keeps him from rocking the boat, so he refuses to try something new. This conflict between longing and security must be resolved. Professionals do this by merging their

---

[1] T.O.M.A.S.-Prinzip® is a protected trademark owned by Liscia Consulting and registered with the German Patent and Trademark Office.

daring with their need for security. The hero's *journey ritual* was formulated by the US American author and psychologist Paul Rebillot[1] and aids change managers in dissolving their workers' personal resistance and individual barriers.

The major component of *story changing*® is what we call the *story changing*® board, a twelve-step model. Each step describes a location on the path to change.

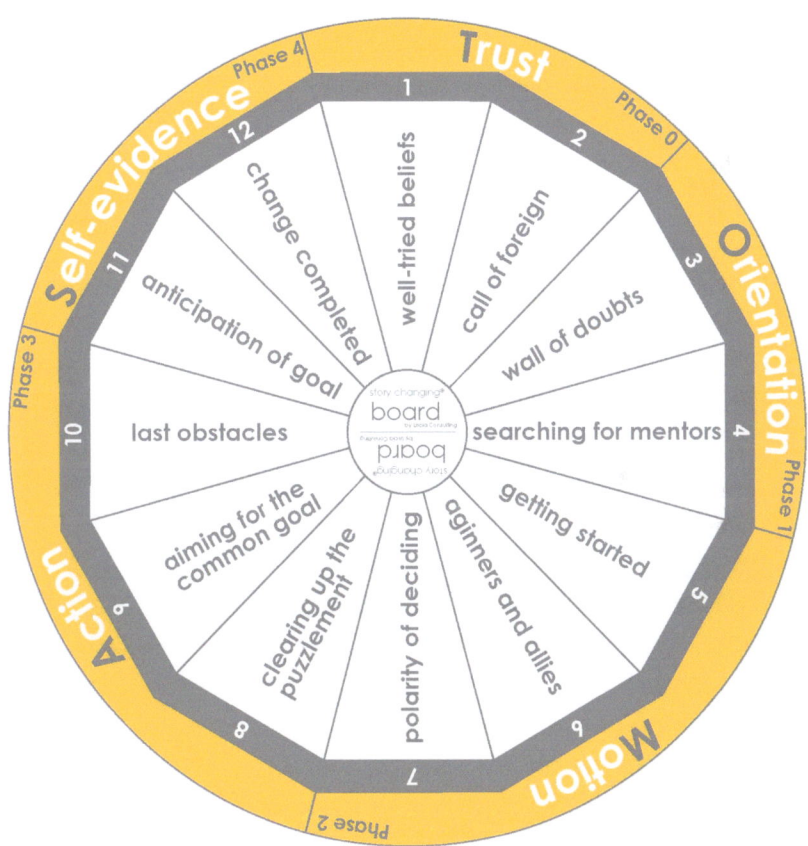

_____

1   Cf. Rebillot, Paul/Kay, Melissa, *The Hero's Journey: A Call to Adventure*, Eagle Books 2017

Step 1	"Well tried beliefs": Here, we find ourselves at the status quo, before any change has taken place. A neutral, external view observes prevailing patterns and convictions that have yet to be questioned.
Step 2	"Call of foreign": Upcoming changes are announced. Since change questions existing paradigms, the reactions differ according to a person's mindset.
Step 3	"Wall of doubts": Those involved are consumed by doubt. They doubt their competence instead of actively seeking solutions. They doubt the process's feasibility (constant contradictions and criticism). They doubt the process's meaningfulness (obstinacy, obtuseness and insisting on stability). They doubt their leaders (suspicion prevails).
Step 4	"Searching for mentors": This is where rejection changes into welcome. Someone must take the lead. This is the mentor who propagates enthusiasm for the process.
Step 5	"Getting started": Taking the first steps on a new path, placing the transition in a new light. Successes are recognized, but there are no winners or losers.
Step 6	"Aginners and allies": This reveals the deterrents and opponents within the company, as well as the cheer leaders and traveling companions.
Step 7	"Polarity of deciding": Now we know the decision leads in the right direction. However, polarity is evident – you can only decide for the change or against the change.
Step 8	"Clearing up the puzzlement": We now respond to any remaining doubts. Responsibility is assumed for the outcome. Inner values are made evident.
Step 9	"Aiming for the common goal": This step puts an end to doubters' attempts to arrest change. Adversaries become travel companions.
Step 10	"Last obstacles": Any externals we depend on are convinced of the transition's necessity.

Step 11   "Anticipation of goal": No longer can anyone imagine not following
            through with the transition. They are dedicated to the path. The
            transition is experienced as a done deed.

Step 12   "Change completed": The transition is concluded. A lessons-learned
            process is launched. What worked well? What didn't? What must
            be taken into account next time around?

We have printed the *story changing*® board on fabrics in a variety of sizes
to hang on the wall or, in a large group, to lay out on the floor. Following the
introductory lecture on the model, each participant is given a round, fabric
marker to lay on the step in the process where he or she believes himself or
herself to be at the moment.

The distribution of markers in the circle is very informative. Some employees
find themselves at the very beginning, while others are in the middle and again
others have nearly completed the process. Although everyone is talking about
the same, concrete situation, each is coming from an entirely different direction,
sending highly varied messages to their team or department.

Precisely these variations in perception make a leader's work during
transitional processes so complex. In the beginning, the leader does not have
his team on the same emotional page, they are distributed throughout the
entire book. The challenge is doubly demanding as he intends to lead his people
through the process while he is in the middle of the transitional process himself.

The *story changing*® board has proven to be an enormous help, making
subjective perceptions visually evident and open for discussion. This is vital for
enabling each employee to be well prepared for the transitional process. Much
too often, changes are instigated with little foresight or dictated by the executive
level outright. In such cases, employees have no opportunity to contribute their
own ideas, and are left on their own when it comes to applying a new software,
for example, or figuring out what lean management means for their own work
area. So, it's no wonder really, when a company's backbone (its workforce)
hasn't a clue as to why change is taking place, they reject it wholesale from the
onset. It's astounding how a lack of communication or a faulty (non-existent)
information strategy can infiltrate an entire company's structure.

Time and again, we witness actions being instigated before the concept has matured and executives have developed a strategy for applying the concept wholesale.

This can only lead to confusion, rumors and speculation, with devastating consequences. The more deficient a company's communication strategy is, the more debilitating an impact it has on efficiency, effectiveness and productivity. Nobody's working because everybody's talking about what might be in store for them. If there are no leaders communicating with their workers, then workers will talk among themselves, mutually exacerbating their insecurity, generating opposition and panic.

When you are looking forward to something, you paint a pleasurable picture of it in your mind's eye. But if your information is vague, plenty of space opens up to imagine the worst, to worry about what might happen – even if these concerns are unfounded. Dale Carnegie, U.S. American author, describes a similar scenario in his book *How to stop worrying and start living*, when a neighbor tried to talk him into getting a smallpox vaccination.

"He was only one of thousands of volunteers who were ringing doorbells all over New York City. Frightened people stood in line for hours to be vaccinated. [...] More than two thousand doctors and nurses worked feverishly day and night, vaccinating crowds. What was the cause of all this excitement? Eight people in New York had smallpox – and two had died. There were two deaths out of a population of almost eight million.

Now, I have lived in New York for many, many years; and no one has ever yet rung my bell to warn me against the emotional sickness of worry – an illness that, during the same period of time, has caused ten thousand times more damage than smallpox. No doorbell ringer has ever warned me that one person out of ten now living in these United States will have a nervous breakdown – induced in the vast majority of cases by worry and emotional conflicts."[1]

Working with the *story changing*® board makes the diffuse solid, minimizing communication misunderstandings on all company levels. When a leader says

---

[1] Carnegie, Dale; *How to stop worrying and start living*, Chapter 3 *What worry may do to you*, page 20 ff. Chaucer Press 1948

at a meeting, "We now need to fully concentrate our energies on step 6," his colleagues all know exactly what he is talking about and how to go about it. It is time to probe into who is against the proposed change and who supports it. All systems go.

It is also useful to apply the *story changing*® board during a transitional process, illustrating the progress made since the initial visualization. When approximately forty employees at an industrial enterprise placed their markers at the beginning of a transitional process, a classic distribution emerged. Some markers were on step 2 and the rest were scattered on steps 3, 4 and 5.

Six months later at the same company, we rolled out the *story changing*® board again and asked the people to place their markers. It was evident that everyone had progressed well down the road, most of the markers laying on step 8 or 9, with a few on step 10, as well. We then projected a photo of the original *story changing*® board visualization, so that participants could see for themselves how far they had come toward completing the transitional progress.

Story changing® can be applied as described above and is equally effective in private, individual coaching. The same questions arise during a person's individual evolution, such as a promotion, as they do in a team, "Where do I stand right now? What will the next step bring and how can I prepare for it? Have I forgotten anything in retrospect?" The *story changing*® board most certainly provides the option to return to the previous step, should something have been overlooked the first time around.

One of the greatest advantages to the *story changing*® board is the security it provides employees for future changes. If you have successfully applied the *story changing*® board one time around, then it will help you again the next time. The tool has become a known entity, something people can rely on. This is a key factor, as we have already mentioned the human resistance to change and to transitional process. Yet, when they recognize the approach, they feel more comfortable with the process.

An employee having already worked with the *story changing*® board, wouldn't need to repeat all the guiding measures. When deemed necessary during the first transitional process, he may have received, for example, stress management coaching or training at step 3. He would not need to repeat this measure the next time, he has already acquired the skills to handle it. We have compiled the measures accompanying each of *story changing®* board steps in the *story changing®* toolbox.

Story changing® is embedded in the *T.O.M.A.S. Principle*[1]. The acronym represents the five phases of change (Trust, Orientation, Motion, Action und Self-evidence) and serves to organize and steer a transitional process. It also gives leaders points of reference for shaping change, depicting the focus of activity during each phase. This could be trust-building measures or initiating the first steps in a transitional process.

In November 2016 in Hamburg, our concept won out over 60 other competitors when we were granted the annual award of the *Deutscher Verband für Coaching und Training e.V.* / German Coaching and Training Association (DVCT). Not only the five-person jury, made up of commercial representatives, gave us their votes, the trade-specific audience also applauded and avouched for our *story changing®* at the final, live presentation.

Since October 2017, we offer training to become a *story changing®* Consultant. Our goal is to qualify our clients to independently carry through transitional processes in-house, without us. We then only need to provide sporadic support. The training takes place over six consecutive days and is completed after twelve months, at the latest, with an in-house certificate.

A story changing® Consultant trained by us is not only a sparring partner in strategy development, he is also equipped to deliver a solid concept for guiding the transitional process. Consultation can begin prior to launching the transitional phase as well as during its initial phase.

Thus, competent transitional process guidance ranges from painting the big picture to carrying out measures such as moderating workshops, training and coaching. Depending on an advisor's training and experience, as well as the scope of a transitional process, a *story changing®* Consultant can carry out the entire process single-handedly or, in agreement with the client, work with moderators, trainers or coaches. A *story changing®* Consultant works with both the *story changing®* board and its toolbox, which, as already mentioned, shows

---

[1] T.O.M.A.S.-Prinzip® is a protected trademark owned by Liscia Consulting and registered with the German Patent and Trademark Office.

precisely what leaders and executives must do, when to do it and how to do it. Subsequently, a detailed plan of action is generated, drawing on well-known instruments such as RASIC und Cynefin Framework. (Detailed information on Cynefin Framework can be read in *Workbook: Education*).

A *story changing*® Consultant offers individuals, leaders and companies an outstanding method for grasping and governing complexities, bypassing chaos and frictional loss.

Key Lisciaman message
Story changing® visualizes the subjective, emotional experiences of an employee during a transitional process, applying the *story changing*® board, a twelve steps model.

Your notes

_____

_____

_____

_____

_____

_____

_____

_____

_____

_____

_____

_____

_____

_____

_____

_____

_____

Worksheet: Which transitional changes are you going through now?

Considering this transitional process, enter you and your colleagues/employees in the story changing® model, using, for example, their initials.
On which step do you find yourself right now?
Where are your colleagues/employees?

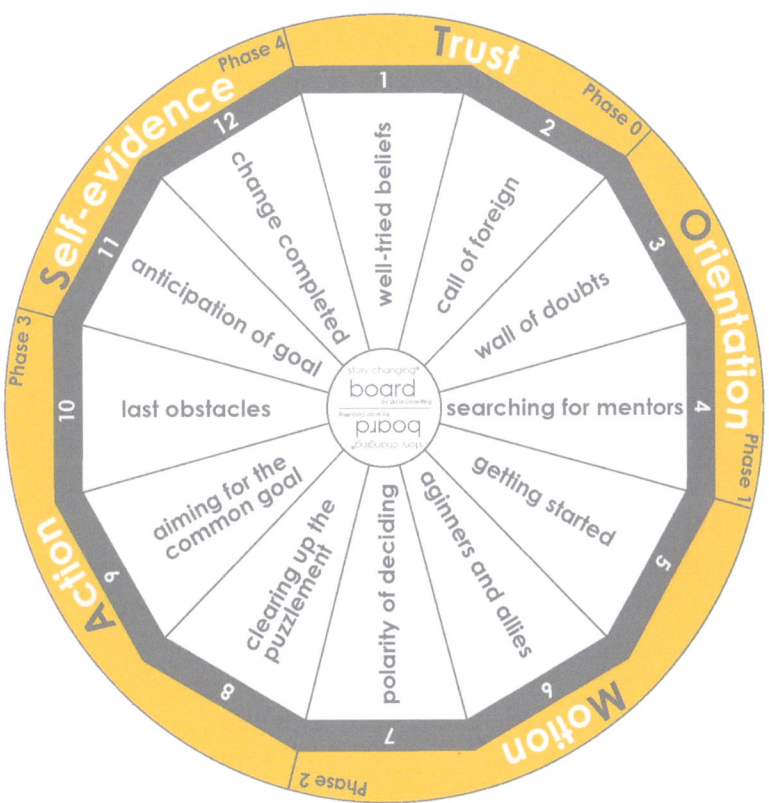

Should you find yourselves on varying steps in the process, probe into why that could be!

What is your current standing on the phases of the T.O.M.A.S.-Principle[1]?

Phase 0 = Trust: How do you inspire, or have inspired, trust?

Phase 1 = Orientation: What shape does your in-house communication take, providing the best possible orientation? Is there more you can do?

Phase 2 = Motion: How do you create goal transparency? Which 'low-hanging fruits' can be harvested?

Phase 3 = Action: How do you promote consistency in achieving goals?

Phase 4 = Self-evidence: What does your lessons-learned process look like? What went well? What went badly? What will you do differently in the next transitional process?

---

[1] T.O.M.A.S.-Prinzip® is a protected trademark owned by Liscia Consulting and registered with the German Patent and Trademark Office.

CEO:	You know, it would be so nice if our workers paid more attention to their health.
LISCIA:	How do you contribute to your workers' health?
CEO:	Oh, we do our bit. Just last year we started a cooperation with a fitness center. Our workers can get a discount on membership fees. But I can't force anyone to go there, now can I?
LISCIA:	No, you can't force them. And what do you do *in-house*?
CEO:	You mean, more than that?
LISCIA:	Yes, I mean something that takes place during work hours, not after work, like the fitness center.
CEO:	Well, you know, I believe my efforts as an employer are limited. In the end, my workers' health practices are none of my business.
LISCIA:	I beg to differ. Let's see if we can't stake those limits – that you most likely set yourself – just a step or two further away.

Cultivating physical and mental resources

There is no doubt about it – health is the greatest human asset. And companies know full well that only healthy people make productive employees. Studies reveal that healthier people are happier workers. Regular exercise, healthful nutrition and stress-releasing activities keep them healthy and alert, resulting in less sick-leave, in heightened motivation and productivity, and in a comfortable work environment. Naturally, every staff member can cultivate her performance potential in her leisure time – but health has long ceased to be a private issue. In the meantime, companies have also become aware of this fact, particularly when considering the enormous leap in burnout cases over the past 15 years and the absenteeism it causes. We have learned that companies are just as responsible for maintaining and boosting employee health as the employees themselves are.

Leaders must be exemplary role models! One of our most important messages in this context is, "Take care of yourself, so you can take care of others." When we ask, who is the most important person in the company, the immediate response is usually, "The customer, of course!" When we shake our heads, many say, "Okay, it must be the workforce." But that's not the answer we're looking for either. The right answer is, "I am. If I don't take proper care of myself, I deplete my resources for taking care of others."

It is a thoroughly irresponsible leader that abuses her physical and/or mental resources. She takes the risk of no longer being able to competently lead her company. This is a common phenomenon we have observed especially in proprietor-run enterprises. When there is but one person at the top, and she ruthlessly exploits her energies, the entire business is threatened with collapse when she must take extended leave of absence due to exhaustion and related health issues.

Unfortunately, we have often made the acquaintance of authoritative, dogmatic Women-at-the-Top who were hell-bent on inspecting every tiny decision, no matter how trifling. Even the final trade fair flyer had to have her okay, despite having a professional marketing and trade fair department. In companies led thusly, there isn't a single leader who remembers what it's like to make an independent decision. We will address this issue in the following chapter.

Ruinous behavior will sooner or later rebound with a vengeance. The longer the overload, ignoring your body's signals without caring for them, the graver the consequences. When the inevitable collapse comes, leaders are usually out of action for months at a time, leaving their business in utter chaos because employees have no idea, or practice in, how to act autonomously.

Turning the tables and repairing damage before it can wreak havoc is best illustrated by Saskia, a manager at a logistics business. Saskia was sent to us to work on stress and burnout syndrome issues. Up until that time, Saskia had spent an average of 17 hours a day at work, usually working weekends as well. She went at her job with dedication and passion, felt good about herself and went to work eagerly. This is quite common on the pathway to burnout, as people are so utterly engaged and enthusiastic, they over-extend their physical and mental resources without giving them a second thought. We'll get back to this subtle process later on in this chapter.

Saskia didn't think much of it when she had a mental, cognitive blackout. It faded quickly. But when she told her husband about it, he recognized it for the symptom it was and asked her to immediately seek out a doctor. The medical examination, however, gave no indication of illness or irregularities. Saskia then spoke with her boss, who sent her to us for coaching. We noticed Saskia's tendency to approach her issues very analytically, which led us to play out the inner team with her. This personality model of plurality, formulated by German psychologist Friedemann Schulz von Thun, assumes each person encompasses a variety of voices, concurring as well as opposing, talking to one another. There is, for example, the go-getter, the decelerator, the courageous, the cautious or the sentinel. And all of them want to be heard.[1]

Together with Saskia, we sketched out her inner team on a whiteboard. Clearly, her go-getter was the dominant voice, striving eagerly for success, shining with customers and ever-ready to stand in the spotlight. The go-getter gave her the momentous drive to master working 17 hours a day. At this point we introduced the topic polarity. If Saskia said *yes* to working 17 hours each day, what did she say *no* to? Which aspects in her life were thoroughly neglected or given little attention? (More on polarity in the next chapter.) Naturally, her family - her husband and two daughters - saw very little of her, and her friendships, care for her health and sports were not even minor priorities.

We approached Saskia with the topic of family, who took on the role of sentinel. "I do, of course, take care of my family" she said. "How, precisely," we probed. "By bringing home enough money, creating a financial basis for a good, secure life. I build and maintain our existential foundation," was her answer. Saskia focused on the second step of the pyramid, her family's financial security. A lack of free time caused her to neglect the social needs (step 3).

"If you are the sentinel for your family, who takes care of you?" we now wanted to know. Saskia was unable to answer the question. "I don't have a sentinel," she said. Together, we reached the conclusion that Saskia needed to introduce the sentinel to her inner team, creating someone whose job it was to watch over her, blowing the horn when she once more ignored her body's warning signals. Otherwise, she risked burnout or some other illness. A cognitive blackout is nothing to trifle with, it must be taken seriously. Saskia realized she was obligated to take better care of herself, otherwise, eventually,

---

[1] Cf. Schulz von Thun, Friedemann, *Talking to Each Other, Book 3: The Inner Team* (not available in English), Rowohlt Taschenbuch Verlag 2013

she wouldn't be able to take care of her family. Illness would step in, severing the cord between work and providing her family's existential foundation. We now went on to develop measures, which would be patrolled by the inner sentinel. One principal element was restructuring Saskia's team and developing her co-workers. Several of whom she had held at arm's length for years while their talents wasted away. Saskia had to do everything herself. Most of them, however, were well equipped to take on more responsibility and were champing at the bit when the opportunity finally arrived. Saskia could now throttle her workload and spend more time with her family. She also took markedly better care of herself, doing sports regularly, improving the quality of her diet and going out with friends.

It was wonderful to experience Saskia's openness to coaching and her consistency in following through with the measures we had developed together. She distinctly improved her quality of life, timely and successfully skirting a looming collapse and long-term absence from work. Unfortunately, initial burnout warning signals are most often ignored or escape notice altogether. We see one reason being the burnout process's subtlety, its slow, gradual invasion. Rarely does burnout hit you like a Mack truck, most people admit they haven't been sleeping well for quite some time, had colds or infections more often or weren't able to unwind over weekends. These signals are usually put down to a temporary phase, that will surely pass quickly.

You could compare the process to a frog that is about to be cooked. If you put the frog in boiling water, it will simply jump back out again. Frogs can do that, you know, their feet allow them to practically jump over water. So, the frog wouldn't stay in hot water, but make tracks for freedom. (Unless, of course the pot was very tall.) but if you were to place the frog in cold water and increase the temperature slowly, it will enjoy the warmth spreading around it and never even realize it is being cooked.

In social psychology, this phenomenon is called *shifting baseline*. If a person is required to immediately change her behavior, acting in a way that is detrimental to her well-being, she would in all probability say, "No way, thank-you. That's not for me." But if you break down the process into 100 or 1,000 tiny steps, the reaction is completely different. This person would take on each of these steps without the ghost of resistance because the change is so gradual - in homeopathic doses - and barely perceptible. A transition taken in baby steps causes us to accept changes we would normally and thoroughly reject if they were to occur in one giant step.[1]

Burnout follows the same principle. You launch a project with vim and vigor or take on a new position and the stress level is well within the tolerance range. Over time, however, the burden increases in weight. Not all at once, but steadily, step by step. This is what a manager told us when his company appointed him to manage an ailing plant in southern Europe. The position was supposedly limited to half a year, just enough time to pull the cart out of the mud, but after three years the crisis still wasn't surmounted. The manager's onus and accompanying stress grew consistently over this time. "If I had begun the job with this stress level, I would have collapsed immediately," he told us. But, similar to the frog, the heat increased gradually, hardly noticeably, so the situation was initially enjoyable. The sum total of countless tiny steps led, and leads, to burnout.

At some point, you are literally pulled up short at the end of the road. This was true for Miriam Meckel, communications scientist, Germany's youngest professor, government speaker and TV moderator, when she collapsed in 2008.

"Up until then, Miriam Meckel had spent the past fifteen years of her life in the fast lane, rushing from one continent to the next. [...] She moderated one last event in Berlin [...] and when she awoke the next morning she was unable to leave her bed. She was beset with pain, attacks of profuse sweating and could do nothing but sit there and weep. And then she did something she still cannot grasp. Although she was wholly incapacitated, couldn't even lift her suitcase, she sat down at her computer to read her emails. When she discovered fifty new emails in her mailbox, she fell apart completely. Her wife, TV moderator Anne Will, brought her to a doctor who lost no time in making the obvious diagnosis - severe exhaustion coupled with an infection. No one had thought it possible, least of all herself, but the fact was, Miriam Meckel had run out of steam."[2]

---

[1] Cf. zeit.de, *Gestern böse, heute normal / Yesterday testy, today normal*, 17.05.2017

[2] faz.de, *Diagnose: Totale Erschöpfung, Miriam Meckels Burnout-Buch / Total Exhaustion, Miriam Meckel's Burnout Book*, 10.03.2010

For this reason, leaders neglecting their physical and mental resources and/ or those failing to address this issue with their employees, do not merit their leadership. They are irresponsible. This includes their use of language. We run interference the moment we heard someone say, "We expect our workers to give 100 percent, all the time."

Why this statement raises our hackles can be clearly illustrated with the battery metaphor. Our first generation of notebooks had a warning function whenever the battery power was down to ten percent. The battery must then be recharged. If we allowed it to fall down to zero power, the battery would fail completely and could not be repaired. (This happened once, so we speak from experience!) More modern devices simply shut down automatically to avoid irreparable battery damage.

Thus, we urge those responsible to grant their employees the same attentiveness that they give their notebook or smartphone batteries. Employers should not expect 100 percent performance from their workers unless they want to run the risk of total discharge without hope of repair. There's no need to demand 100 percent. Be happy and respectful receiving 90 percent, and that continuously. Your employees need the other ten percent to rejuvenate and recharge their batteries.

Many companies, however, are tapping in the dark when it comes to determining which measures are effective for everyday health management, adding value to all areas of workers' lives. To shed light on the matter, we developed the *A.P.F.E.L. Strategy*[1] , the acronym standing for Activity, Pauses, Fitness, Eating practices and Living power. The *A.P.F.E.L. Strategy* provides businesses with an effective, holistic concept for maintaining their staff members' health, body and soul.

It begins at the beginning, with the letter A as in Activity. Recent scientific studies prove that mental acuity is just as dependent on physical exercise as it is on mind jogging. Daily office work offers a goodly number of easy-to-execute options promoting staffers' well-being within a few minutes. Our *A.P.F.E.L. Strategy* shows you specific invigorating and relaxing exercises at the desk,

---

[1]   The A.P.F.E.L.-Strategie® is a protected trademark owned by Liscia Consulting and registered with the German Patent and Trademark Office.

as well as guidance in installing mini-activities "on the side." Here's just one example: Printers should be installed in a separate room, compelling office staff to get up and retrieve their printouts. Also, a little miracle worker is the ten to fifteen-minute walk during lunch hour, clearing minds and relaxing bodies, invigorating them for the second half of the workday. A short walk is also the ideal refresher for computer-weary eyes.

This brings us directly to the next letter in the *A.P.F.E.L. Strategy*, namely P for Pauses. One of the most neglected aspects, pauses are often 'forgotten' or foregone due to a time crunch. Yet, we have all noticed how our effectiveness deteriorates when we can no longer concentrate. A full cup will not hold any more water, it simply overflows. At some point, we are so keyed up and overloaded that it's useless to try and keep working, but we can't relax at home, either.

"Studies show that short, recuperative phases in the course of a workday cannot be put off for later. 'As fatigue increases throughout the day, we must also increase our efforts,' psychologist Johannes Wendsche says, [...] Which results in intensified exhaustion at the end of the day. A person working non-stop to get more done before she goes home, will most likely not be able to enjoy her evening, but can only lay on the sofa, fully depleted and [...] in the long-term puts her health at serious risk."[1]

It's not about taking long breaks and losing touch with whatever it is you're working on. Short regenerative pauses of two to five minutes are enough to refresh your concentration capacity. Do a few counter-balancing exercises or just open the office window and let in some fresh air. In our *A.P.F.E.L. Strategy* training sessions, we school you in simple, effective methods for giving yourself a moment's respite, refreshing your mind and returning to work energized.

Although the next letter in the acronym stands for Fitness, it is not related to physical activities. Fitness here indicates a reflection or assessment of your ability to meet the demands you or others ask of yourself. Taking the word at its literal meaning of 'ability, skill or strength,' the question to ask yourself is, "Do my physical and mental strengths correspond with my workload demands?"

---

[1] zeit.de, *Mach mal Pause / Take a break*, 24.03.2011

If the answer is no, we join up with the employee to work out customized ways and means to improve her deficient areas, helping her to become better equipped to meet workload demands. These can be "bodybuilding" exercises to increase brain-power or a workplace examination attentive to ergonomic aspects. Eating practices, the E in our *A.P.F.E.L. Strategy*, are the engines that drive a successful work day. We're not talking about losing weight or having a super-model figure, the primary interest is consciously choosing healthy meals and snacks that feed the flow of energy instead of draining the reservoir. Many companies lack the knowledge necessary to create ideal lunches – ones that vitalize and regenerate, instead of leading to performance lows and attacks of fatigue in the afternoon. Yet, one of the most neglected health factors is drinking sufficient liquids throughout the day. Around 75 percent of headaches occurring during the second half of the workday are caused by dehydration, which also triggers ebbing concentration and dizziness.

When all the preceding factors are well accounted for, employees will have decidedly more Living power – the final letter in the *A.P.F.E.L. Strategy*. And this has a direct, positive impact on the enterprise's performance. Every penny spent on company health leads to a significant increase in staff endurance and performance. Studies prove the investment is well worth it, as every dollar invested in company health is returned at least threefold in employee performance.

Thus, businesses are well-advised to make employee health an executive issue. Most importantly, managerial staff must grasp its significance and assume responsibility for their employees' physical and mental strength, as they are the company's most valuable resource. Health is no longer a private matter. Leaders must see to it that employee health is on the daily agenda, actively making time and creating space to address and remedy health issues.

Your employees will appreciate workplace health promotion, as it directly reflects the company's regard for and interest in their workers. A good, well-founded health promotion program can also promote your employer status, attracting a new generation of staff members. In times of specialist shortages, this is not to be underestimated. Especially Generation Y highly value quality of life and health, as Miriam Goos illustrates in her 2014 *Focus* article,

"They are willing to work hard; are effective and motivated. In return, the company is to provide opportunities for personal development and advanced education. This includes not only equal opportunities and increasing flexibility, but also substantial health and performance promotion. Should the company neglect this area, Generation Y feels undervalued and stymied in their personal development."[1]

Generation Z, also known as the Homeland Generation, born after 1995, has also joined the job market, even though most businesses are not aware of it and are still focusing on Generation Y, or Millennials. There is, however, a significant difference between the two. Generation Y defines quality of life as having flexible work hours and job rotation. Homelands, on the other hand, value regular work hours and open-end contracts. This difference must be accounted for when leading cross-generational teams. You will find more on this crucial topic in our books *D.R.E.A.M. of LEADERS® Leadership is not an Illusion* and *Workbook Attitude*.

With our *A.P.F.E.L. Strategy*, we offer companies the opportunity to become qualified in the area of health management. In recognition of our accomplishment, we were awarded the *INDUSTRIEPREIS (Industry Prize) 2011* for a *Qualified Product* in the category Professional Services.

---

[1] focus.de, *"Generation Y": So ticken die jungen Selbstoptimierer / How young self-optimizers tick,*
22.02.2014

Key Lisciaman message
A leader acts irresponsibly when she neglects to care for her physical and mental resources. She must attend to herself first, subsequently ensuring her employees do the same.

Your notes

Worksheet – Test: Am I a burn-out candidate?[1]

Please answer all questions spontaneously, without thinking about them too much. Should you prefer not to write your answers in this book, you may also take the test anonymously online under www.gezeitenhaus.de/burn-out-test. html

	no	some-times	often	yes
1. Do you feel completely bogged down?	0	2	4	6
2. Have you become more irritable?	0	1	2	3
3. Do you take pleasure in your work?	3	2	1	0
4. Are you constantly glum?	0	1	2	3
5. Are you too exhausted for leisure time activities?	0	1	2	3
6. Do you have an increased number of physical complaints?	0	2	4	6
7. Do you find yourself withdrawing from your friends?	0	1	2	3
8. Do you drink alcohol more often than usual?	0	2	4	6

---

[1] Cf. Manfred Nelting, *Burn-out – Wenn die Maske zerbricht. Wie man Überbelastung erkennt und neue Wege geht.* © 2010 Mosaik, München, in der Verlagsgruppe Random House GmbH (not available in English).

9. Do you have hope that things will change?	3	2	1	0
10. Do you have any plans?	3	2	1	0
11. Do you sleep well?	6	4	2	0
12. Do you have time for your partner?	3	2	1	0
13. Do you turn off your cellphone when in company or at other appropriate times?	6	4	2	0
14. Do you feel completely drained?	0	1	2	3
15. Are you haunted by unfamiliar fears?	0	1	2	3
16. Does life seem senseless to you?	0	1	2	3
17. Are you constantly tense and under pressure?	0	1	2	3
18. Does your partner or do your friends support you?	6	4	2	0
19. Do you feel pauses are just a waste of time?	0	1	2	3
20. Do you take sleeping pills or sedatives?	0	1	2	3

Evaluation:

Add up the numbers in the boxes you have checked. Referring to the results below, find the area corresponding to the sum you've totaled. Read the text and as the case may be, speak about these results with a competent person, i.e. your family doctor.

0-15 Points:

Congratulations! You meet your challenges with effective strategies, tending your life and surroundings well.

16-34 Points:

Take preventative steps against burn-out. There are plenty of options, use them!

35-49 Points:

You are a burn-out candidate. Be aware that burn-out symptoms are insidious, and you can still react! Seek professional advice from your doctor, a psychologist or coach.

50-78 Points:

You run a high burn-out risk or are well on your way to burning out. The sooner you courageously face this fact, the more quickly you will receive effective help and the necessary treatment. Seek professional advice from your doctor, a psychologist or coach.

CEO:	My colleague is also a leader, but he refuses to make decisions.
LISCIA:	What if I told you there's no such thing as not deciding?
CEO:	I don't get it.
LISCIA:	If your colleague doesn't make decisions, then he decides to let things remain as they are. The question is, is he aware of it?
CEO:	There's no reason to avoid making decisions.
LISCIA:	Everyone has their reasons for what they do, fear, intrigue, higher priorities, pressure, to name just a few."
CEO:	Yeah, fear might have something to do with it…

Making decisions

A leader is always a decider. Particularly in times of transition, he must be equipped to make active decisions to urge the process forward. Yet, every decision carries responsibility for the resulting consequences. We have learned that assuming responsibility for their decisions is what provokes most leaders into delaying the decision-making process – the more far-reaching the possible impact, the longer they hesitate.

But hoping that things will work themselves out if you just wait long enough – *ignore it and it will go away* – is a coward's strategy. And rarely works. There is no such thing as *not* deciding. If a leader does not make a choice, he has chosen to vegetate instead of act, and for this, too, he is responsible.

This situation is comparable to *Buridan's ass*, an allegory introduced by the Persian philosopher Al-Ghazālī (1058-1111), wherein a hungry ass is placed between two equally large and equally distant piles of hay. Unable to decide which hay it should eat first; the ass dies of starvation.[1]

A solar technology business in Thuringia provides a good example in this context. Two brothers, Thomas and Jens, founded the company shortly before the turn of the century. The first few years showed steady growth – particularly the Renewable Energies Act (EEG) in 2000 brought on a renewable energy boom as it regulated the preferred grid infeed of electricity from renewable energy sources, providing producers with a guaranteed commission rate. The

---

[1] Cf. https://en.wikipedia.org/wiki/Buridan's_ass

brothers' business also caught the wave, employing over 100 workers at peak periods.

When China entered the market with ever-cheaper solar and photovoltaic modules and state subsidizing was dramatically cut in 2012, things changed dramatically. We came to the business in Thuringia as commissions were going belly-up and the brothers were forced to let go of nearly half of their workforce. Jens was the one who called on us, as he read the writing on the wall and was ready for a change. He was hoping his brother would listen to external advice after he had already broached numerous options, only to have them nipped in the bud one by one. Thomas stonewalled. He was adept at ignoring the change in parameters. It was blatantly obvious that something had to give. The employees were also ready and willing, but Thomas was simply incapable of taking decisive action. In contrast to Jens, he refused to look reality in the eye, his decision was to merely sit the crisis out.

Together with Jens, we had managed to develop promising measures, giving the enterprise a new direction. Until that point, the Thuringia company's major target group was customers with large surfaces, such as barn roofs on farms or public buildings like schools and administrative structures, where in one go a large number of solar panels could be sold and installed. When subsidizing was cut, customers lost interest - it simply wasn't worth it anymore.

In any case, there was still good money to be made installing solar panels or photovoltaic on private homes. Our plan was to redirect the company to this target group and suggested, among other things, developing an app with which employees could make direct, efficient contact with potential customers. All they had to do was photograph a prospective house with their tablets and within seconds the app would calculate the number of solar modules, determine their optimal position and generate a composite photo, depicting the house once the modules were in place.

Together with Jens, we were thoroughly convinced the tablet photo was a brilliant tool for winning new customers. The company's sales staff could photograph private homes with appropriate southern exposure, approach home owners directly, show them exactly what they could do with their roof, providing answers to questions on costs and benefits. There couldn't be a more effective sales opener! As a Swiss company found out later, successfully applying this app.

Unbelievable as it may seem, Thomas rejected all arguments. They went in one ear and out the other. He held tight to his inertia, not even asserting his company's pending claims. Unpaid incoming revenues, amounting to an unheard-of six-digit sum, gathered dust on his desk, while his company was on the brink of bankruptcy! No one else was permitted to write invoices, but he *hadn't gotten around to it*, when we asked.

Yet, there's more. Fifty percent of the commission for our consultation was sponsored by the European Social Fund. But Thomas failed to meet the application deadline, thereby forfeiting his claim to funds. He held us responsible, claiming we neglected to inform him of the deadline, which of course, wasn't true. He demanded we pay him the lost funds. Naturally, we turned him down and despite his audacity, made him one last offer. "We can't give you back your money. The only thing we can offer you is one day free of charge to get the ball rolling, but under one condition - you come prepared to work with us in earnest, productively and prepared to make firm decisions. You know where to find us and we're ready to get to work with you."

We never heard from him again. Shortly thereafter, his brother Jens informed us he had resigned from the company, as it was going nowhere fast. We were very sad to hear that, since, with the appropriate measures, the enterprise had enormous potential to reclaim its former strength. Instead, another twenty employees were let go…

Although Thomas apparently was incapable of making decisions, he did decide - subconsciously - to stagnate. His inertia contributed *decisively* to *not* redirect his company. He not only blocked major decisions, he also couldn't or wouldn't delegate minor movements, giving the downward spiral added momentum. It would have been no skin off his nose if he were to, for example, allow someone else to write invoices to ensure the company's liquidity.

Our experience reveals that it is often the alleged trivialities that should be addressed firmly and immediately to avoid a domino effect triggering severe consequences. In the 1980s, U.S. American sociologists James Q. Wilson und George L. Kelling developed the *Broken Windows Theory*, proposing direct action as a method to combat destruction and escalating criminality in city neighborhoods. The theory applied the accessible image of a broken window, which must be immediately repaired.

"Broken windows theory had an enormous impact on police policy throughout the 1990s and remained influential into the 21st century. Perhaps the most notable application of the theory was in New York City under the direction of Police Commissioner William Bratton. He and others were convinced that the aggressive order-maintenance practices of the New York City Police Department were responsible for the dramatic decrease in crime rates within the city during the 1990s."[1]

Despite the controversial nature of the *Broken Windows Theory*, we approve of taking a zero-tolerance approach in businesses, as well. When there is no decisiveness in trivial cases; when there are no guiding rules for certain activities or no consequences for misdeeds, then employees will not feel obligated to follow major rules. Remember the southeast European business at the beginning of this workbook? For over 30 years, they allowed their buildings to fall into neglect. Prior to renovating, the buildings had to be cleared of 30 years of accumulated garbage. Every nook and cranny were used as a dump - old packaging, long obsolete tools, dried out paint cans. The attitude behind this behavior was easy to understand, "If my employer could care less how it looks in here, letting the place go to the dogs, then why should I bother to clean up after myself?" This attitude changed once the place had been thoroughly renovated. Employees were so appreciative of their new work environment that they only left for the day after the place was once more spic and span.

When addressing the topic of decision-making, we like to draw on the law of polarity in physics. Polarity is the position of two diametrically opposed points (poles) within a given space. Batteries, for example, have a positive pole and a negative pole, both are mandatory in order for energy to flow. Positive/positive may sound better, but without the negative, there is no flow. Polarity, also known as the principle of duality, is absolutely everywhere because humanity perceives the world in duality. We divide reality into good/bad, right/wrong, hot/cold, poor/rich, strong/weak, and so on.

---

[1]   https://www.britannica.com/topic/broken-windows-theory

Each 'yes' implies per se a 'no.' When I say, "I will be working longer today." I simultaneously infer, "No, my dear, we won't be able to go shopping together." When coaching, we feel compelled to contradict leaders who say they have trouble saying 'no.' "You don't have a problem saying 'no,' your problem is that you say 'yes'."

You need to consider why you are saying 'yes,' and locate the opposing position. What are the consequences of my agreement?

The manager Saskia said 'yes' to working 17 hours a day. The consequence or antithesis of this decision was little time for her family and for taking care of herself, not to mention neglecting her employees' potential. Only when you take the opposing position into account, can you fully absorb the impact of your decision. When no one loses, as in a win-win situation, then everyone has won. But this conclusion is a fallacy. If there is a winner, then there must be a loser. No matter what you do, no matter what you decide, the opposite option is always there. You are obligated to keep this in mind, since you are responsible for the consequences of your decisions.

Several years ago, the nursing management of a rehab clinic made an appointment with us. When we asked what she was looking for, she answered, "My team is simply not working effectively. I need some serious landscaping here, I need someone willing to cut down trees." Now that was a statement to work with! So, we went to work, established the lay of the land and could soon present the nursing manager with our plan of action. We were well aware that some rather radical changes were in store for some team members, a natural repercussion when you cut down trees, what we were asked to do. It was also more than evident that employees unwilling to accept the changes would have to leave the clinic. Initially, the nursing manager was thrilled with our suggestions. We were to relate them in their entirety to the team and immediately carry through with the first measures.

Yet as the team learned of our plans, it closed ranks against the manager and lodged a complaint with the clinic executives. We had foreseen this or similar resistance and prepared the manager accordingly. But when subjected to pressure from the executive level, she immediately turned tail, promising not to implement the plan. She came back to us saying, "Most of my team went complaining to my boss and now I'm in an uncomfortable predicament. Can we cancel the landscaping project and just plant a few flowers?"

We refused and withdrew from the collaboration. Firstly, we couldn't explain a change of course to the team without losing credibility. Secondly, we are definitely not cosmetic surgeons. The rehab clinic team will continue to be unproductive as long as the nursing management is unwilling to make unpopular decisions.

Many leaders are more than aware of the responsibility, which why they have such a tough time taking a decisive stand. They know that giving a team member an especially delicate assignment means he receives a better status, more prestige and more attention. This decision equally implies that the other team members will not receive these boons. Thus, the leader holds back because they fear the decision is unfair.

"No, it's not unfair," we correct him. "You cannot give the same task to each team member. First off, that is ridiculous and impossible. Secondly, it's leveling down. You are making a conscious decision, well thought through and based on solid arguments. You know your team well enough to deem precisely this worker best for the assignment. The process of elimination is intrinsic to any decision, there's no way around it." A responsible leader must have the self-assurance to endure such a situation. If he doesn't, he's incapacitated. He is unfit to lead.

In global leadership, the international dimension must also be taken into account when it comes to making decisions, i.e. who makes which decisions within which cultural milieu and upon which basis these decisions are made. While it is customary in Germany to discuss a problem collectively, reaching a decision in consensus, things are done differently in the U.S.A. There, information may flow bottom-up, allowing team members to make suggestions, but the actual decision is made top-down, without soliciting consensus from the team. Many are unaware of this as they assume an egalitarian hierarchy and organizational structure is synonymous with democratic decision-making.

"Many executives and managers assume that in more hierarchical societies, decisions will be made at the top by the boss, and in more egalitarian cultures, decisions will be reached by group consensus. Yet on a worldwide scale, we find that hierarchies and decision-making methods are not always correlated. [...] American business culture has become more and more egalitarian over recent decades, but consensual decision making is clearly not the norm. [...] Contrast that with what happens in Germany, Japan, the Netherlands, and Sweden. If you've collaborated with companies in those countries, you might have noticed that a lot of people seem to be involved in the decision-making process, and it takes a long time to negotiate group agreement."[1]

Furthermore, the word *decision* is grasped in a variety of ways depending on cultural understanding. A consensual decision made in Germany after seemingly endless discussion is then written in stone. It is rarely modified. In the States things look differently.

"American companies favor quick and flexible decisions, so decision-making power is vested in the individual (usually the boss). [...] With a [...] belief that *any decision is better than no decision*. [...] In top-down decision-making cultures, decisions are made quickly, but they are subject to change as new input or arguments arise. When people in these cultures say they've reached a decision, the decision is not a firm commitment but a placeholder that can later be adjusted."[2]

A global leader must keep these differences in mind when working with an international team. (Read more on international teams in our books *D.R.E.A.M. of LEADERS® Leadership is not an Illusion* and *Workbook: Attitude*). He must understand from the outset that his German team, for example, needs more time to arrive at a consensual agreement, but the decision is then final. In the U.S.A., teams may make suggestions, but it is the leader who is expected to make decisions quickly. These decisions, however, are provisional place-holders.

---

[1]   Harvard Business Review, *Being the Boss in Brussels, Boston, and Beijing,* July-August 2017
[2]   Ibid.

Key Lisciaman message
A leader must be able to make decisions and prepared to bear responsibility for the resulting consequences. There is no such thing as not deciding – when someone does not decide, he decides in favor of the status quo.

Your notes

Worksheet: Tetralemma – A decision-making method

The tetralemma (four views) principle comes from ancient Indian Buddhism. In contrast to age-old occidental true/false thinking, tetralemma allows for true or false, true and false, neither true nor false. Thus, there are promptly four approaches to viewing a given situation. An additional, fifth option is none of the above, moving beyond the tetralemma and the context of the four views.

Here's an illustrative example:

Maria's leader asked her if she would like to go to China for a year. Up until a few years ago, Maria would have jumped at the chance; foreign travel is always edifying and looks great on your résumé, to boot. But right now, Maria and her husband are planning to have children, so the timing is less than optimal. Which possibilities can Maria draw from the tetralemma?

A: Go to China
B: Don't go to China (stay put)
A&B: Both go and don't go to China (lead the team virtually and only travel when necessary)
Neither A nor B: Develop someone to go to China in her stead, consciously running the risk of being transferred to a department more suitable for family life.

None of the above, beyond the tetralemma: Take the opportunity to reflect on her professional life and perhaps set out in a completely new direction, i.e. fulfilling a long-treasured dream of opening a coffee house or writing a book, etc.

Which decision demands your attention?
Which of the five decision-making options do you have?
If there is no decision to make, reflect on a past decision. Which additional options would this model have afforded you?

A

A&B

B

~~A&B~~

None of the four views

X

CEO:	I read your article about the Three P's. What were they again? Something with people...party...peccadillo?
LISCIA:	No, but you're getting there. The article dealt with the three dimensions of sustainability: People, Planet, Profit.
CEO:	Yes, that's it! But I thought sustainability was more of an environmental issue.
LISCIA:	It often is. The article, however, dealt with a fourth dimension we've added to the list – sustaining principles. One more P to pop, if you will.

Sustainability

When we talk about leadership responsibility, we are addressing a vital aspect of sustainability. This means present tense needs should be satisfied without compromising the future generation's ability to meet their needs as well. According to the United Nations Commission on Environment and Development, it is important that the three dimensions of sustainability – social justice, environmental protection and economic efficiency – are given equal attention.

These three dimensions of sustainability are often summed up as *People, Planet, Profit*. In the context of leadership responsibility, we add a fourth dimension – *Principles*. By dint of their position, leaders are obligated to ensure certain principles endure, even amidst changes.

The best-selling author, U.S. American Stephen Covey, spoke of this as *principle-centered leadership*. Paraphrasing his definition, "...when everything is constantly churning and changing, every single person must have something inside them that guides their decisions. And that is their principles."[1]

Leaders are role models. They are responsible for firmly upholding principles, and ensuring they are also upheld by their company or team. Principles are the beacon of orientation for your co-workers. When employees witness your authentic principled behavior, your genuine strength of character, it will give them a sense of security, especially during transitional phases. Principles are not to be confused with values. Values can and must evolve with the times and circumstances. You can read more detailed information on values in our books

---

[1]   Cf. Covey, Stephen R., *The 8th Habit: from Effectiveness to Greatness*, Free Press, 2004

D.R.E.A.M. of LEADERS® *Leadership is not an Illusion* and *Workbook: Attitude*. Principles, however, such as honesty and reliability are intrinsic constants, before, during and after a transition.

When recruiting leaders, principles are also a vital factor. The challenge facing any company aiming for sustainable activity is how quickly the new leader can come into her own. The best way to accelerate a new leader's success is to ensure she embodies the same principles her future employer maintains and needs.

It can, however, due to altered parameters, come about that a company must adapt their values to the new situation. In this case, they must recruit leaders that uphold the desired prospective values, and not the current ones. All the same, it must be understood that success in this case comes more slowly. When new values are applied, then with enduring impact so that they are also valid beyond the current transition. And that takes time. We are often asked how that works. Our answer, "With diligence, patience, stamina and emphasis - otherwise these values are short-lived."

Our basic principles are primarily formed in the first six or seven years of our lives. Ergo, when a leader is in her mid-forties, her principles are nearly 40 years old and correspondingly stable. When these principles are to change, she needs a goodly stretch of time. It is simpler to hire the leader who embodies today the principles I need tomorrow and has already been upholding them for forty years. He will successfully represent and pass on precisely these principles.

Consequently, we can only reiterate our appeal to companies: Direct your recruiting strategy toward a candidate's principles and values instead of concentrating on field competence and/or experience. The fact of the matter is, our principles and values are the main engine driving our behavior. If my first priority as an employer is the compatibility of a candidate's principles and values with my own, and not her field competence, I will discover that transitions are not only easier and more firmly implemented, they are also more successful.

Key Lisciaman message
Leaders must ensure that principles
and values are deeply embedded
within their company and have an
enduring influence, providing
orientation for your employees in
times of constant change.

Your notes

Worksheet: Your principles

What are your principles?

_____
_____
_____
_____

Where, by whom and how are your principles reflected in your professional and private lives?

_____
_____
_____
_____
_____

Where do you find discrepancies between your professional/private life and your principles?

_____
_____
_____
_____
_____

How do you handle these discrepancies?

_____
_____
_____
_____
_____

How do you relate your principles to your employees?

_____

_____

_____

_____

_____

The Authors

Marcello, Gianni and Jan Liscia (left to right)

Since its inception in 2000, taking shape in Paderborn, Germany, the name *Liscia Consulting* has gained ground on both national and international terrain with their excellent work in leader development. A most competent partner for strategy, conception and getting things done.

Business leaders Gianni, Marcello and Jan Liscia are not your everyday seminar conductors. Nor are they generic trainers or coaches. Gianni, Marcello and Jan Liscia are consultants who train and coach *leaders*. They are strategic partners, guiding and mediating transitional processes.

www.Liscia-Consulting.com

Keynote presentations for your event

On the pulse of change with inspiring keynote lectures! A keynote presentation can be designed to run 30 minutes or up to 3 hours – according to your event's agenda!

Together, we determine the focus of your D.R.E.A.M. of LEADERS® keynote lecture, i.e. Employee Engagement in Global Leadership, Transitional Process Leadership or Digital Leadership. Our multifarious and unusual approach infuses your business with new impulses, creating an atmosphere of awakening and a desire for change.

A rational/emotional composition coupled with the blunt, stark reality of our times invokes profound reflection. To easier digest discomfiting truth, we served it with a healthy portion of humor.

One 'n' Herman, the artist

Herman, illustrator

Herman is, and has been for some time, one of the most high-profile, successful pop art painters of our time. His edgy, idiosyncratic graphics and pictures are downright bodacious. Once a trained screen printer, his unleashed creativity has astonished viewers at over 200 national and international exhibits. Herman has been an independent artist since 1991.

Over the past years, the name Herman can also be found under cartoons drawn for a variety of German publishing houses. His *flying heart* comic strip in *Bravo*, a German youth magazine, was published several consecutive years, becoming a household name. The same can be said of the 18 Herman collector's glasses commissioned by *Ritzenhoff*. In 2007, bids were made for 49 Herman paintings at a charity auction benefiting the Peter Maffay Foundation.

www.Kuenstler-Herman.de

**Want more? Here's an overview of all books
by Gianni, Jan & Marcello Liscia:**

Gianni, Jan & Marcello Liscia

D.R.E.A.M.
of
LEADERS

Leadership is not an Illusion

Illustrations:
Herman Reichold

ISBN: 978-3-744-88271-2 – 19,90 € (D), E-Book: 14,99 € (D)

Gianni, Jan & Marcello Liscia

WORKBOOK
DEDICATION

Dedication to the work at hand, with heart and soul,
24 hours a day

Illustrations:
Herman Reichold

ISBN: 978-3-7528-5787-0 – 8,90 € (D), E-Book: 4,99 € (D)

Gianni, Jan & Marcello Liscia

WORKBOOK
EDUCATION

Personal and employee education

Illustrations:
Herman Reichold

ISBN: 978-3-7528-5826-6 – 8,90 € (D), E-Book: 4,99 € (D)

Gianni, Jan & Marcello Liscia

WORKBOOK
ATTITUDE

A question of personal attitude and values which are
lived and experienced

Illustrations:
Herman Reichold

ISBN: 978-3-7528-5827-3 – 8,90 € (D), E-Book: 4,99 € (D)

Gianni, Jan & Marcello Liscia

WORKBOOK
MOTIVATION

Being ready to perform is the basis for all action

Illustrations:
Herman Reichold

ISBN: 978-3-7528-5828-0 – 8,90 € (D), E-Book: 4,99 € (D)

Gianni, Jan & Marcello Liscia

The Book of Happiness

A work and reflection diary

Illustrations:
Herman Reichold

ISBN: 978-3-7528-5829-7 – 8,90 € (D)

All of our titles are available as ebooks (except The Book of Happiness) and can be enjoyed in the German language, too!